SELECT ACTS

John Bessarion,

Cardinal-Bishop of Nicaea

Translated by: D.P. Curtin

Dalcassian Publishing Company
PHILADELPHIA, PA

Copyright @ 2008 Dalcassian Publishing Company

All rights reserved. No part of this publication may be reproduced, distributed, or transmitted in any form or by any means, including photocopying, recording, or other electronic or mechanical methods, without the prior written permission of the publisher, except in the case of brief quotations embodied in critical reviews and certain other non-commercial uses permitted by copyright law. For permission request, write to Dalcassian Publishing Company at dalcassianpublishing at gmail.com

ISBN: 979-8-8691-5857-4 (Paperback)

Library of Congress Control Number:
Author: Curtin, D.P. (1985-)

Printed by Ingram Content Group, 1 Ingram Blvd, La Vergne, Tennessee

First printing edition 2008.

SELECT ACTS

SELECT ACTS

BESSARION CARDINALIS NICENVS
PATRIARCHA CONSTANTINOP.
Non tibi sit laudi sanctum celebrasse Platonem,
Castaque Socraticæ frena pudicitiæ;
Verum quod per te migrauit Græcia Romam,
Et didicit Latios Attica Musa sonos.

SELECT ACTS

ACT I

Bessarion, by divine mercy, bishop of Tusculan, SR of the Cardinal of the Church, in the city of Bononia and exarchate of Ravennate and Romandiole, legate of the apostolic see from the Lateran to his beloved son, archpriest of the collegiate church of Saint Damian of the diocese of Saxenat, eternal peace in the Lord. From the office of legation assigned to us, as it is decent and appropriate, we willingly aim at that by which the poverty of the churches, especially of the cathedrals, and the needs of those antistites in terms of subsidization are provided for in a timely manner, so that they can more easily bear the burdens incumbent upon them to maintain their state decently. Of course, as part of the reverent father in Christ, the petition of Lord Maxianus, bishop of

Saxenatensis, recently presented to us, contained that his Church of Saxenatensis, of which he is recognized as presiding, was and still is in the annual income so small and scanty, that he is not worth at all, according to the propriety of his state, himself and those who serve him conveniently to support And when in his diocese there is a church, or a rural town, called St. Mary Romagnani, but in habit, and not actually cared for, established in forests and wild places, until now vacant by the death of Sempliciani, formerly a canon of Saxenatensis, also known as the 'Martyrdom of Saints', formerly also of the said church, the canons of Saxena, the last rectors of the said church, or of the people, therefore, out of a special grace of subsidizing aid, we would like to assist them, and we would agree to permanently unite and incorporate the aforesaid people into the episcopal church of the said Saxena. We, therefore, who with unwearied studies favored the execution, especially of the pious, just and honest, of the aforesaid people of St. Mary, whose fruits, according to common estimation, do not exceed the annual value of fifteen pounds of gold from the chamber, as the same bishop asserts, and as it is supposed to be vacant. Or, otherwise, it is in any way from any other person who is said to be vacant, unless he has been vacant for such a time that his contribution or provision according to the statutes of the Lateran council has been legitimately devolved to the apostolic see, even if by the constitution which begins Exsecrabilium, vacant! Some cases, whose status is here, for we wish to have it expressly, with all its rights and appurtenances, subject to the episcopal legation of the said church of Saxena, and to every other authority by which we act, we permanently unite, annex and incorporate, deciding that the aforesaid bishop and his successors may grant the aforesaid church of St. Mary, with the said church for the people of Saxena, to keep lawfully and freely in perpetual times, and to receive all the fruits and revenues, and to receive each one with integrity, according to the synodal constitutions of the said Church of Saxena, and not of the provincials, or to the canons and chapters of the said Church of Saxena, the provision or presentation of the rector shall belong, and to the rest who do the contrary, notwithstanding any, all of which we derogate from our own motion and from certain knowledge. Elected that it should now be null and void, if otherwise it happens to be attempted by anyone, knowingly or unknowingly.

Accordingly, we entrust and command the aforesaid tenor of the present to your discretion, inasmuch as you, or another or others, the same bishop or his representative, receiving in his name, the receiver into the bodily possession of the said Church of Saint Mary, and the rights and appurtenances of the same, and you shall defend what has been brought in by our authority, removed thenceforth by any to the unlawful detainer, cause the said bishop or his agent to be admitted to the same church, according to the custom, and to himself or his agent to answer fully for all the fruits, revenues and proceeds, rights and obstacles, checking the contradictors by ecclesiastical censure and other legal remedies.

 Given at Bologna on January 6, 1453.

ACT II

Bessarion, by divine mercy, cardinal of the holy Roman Church, bishop of Tusculan, legate of the apostolic see on the side in the city of Bologna, vicar general of the exarchate of Ravenna and the province of Romandiole in spiritual and temporal matters, reverend in Christ the Father Lord Bishop Regin, and beloved in Christ the sons of the chapter of the same church, greetings in the Lord, et cetera. When it is demanded of us, that which befits honesty and gives way to the honor of churches, especially cathedrals, it is fitting for us to grant it to those who wish, and to impart protection to the wishes of those who ask. Since then, just as your petition contained the series offered to us, you, the aforesaid lord bishop Regin, together with your canons, for the honor of the said church, have led to the imitation of other cathedral churches to establish that every canon of the said church should use the alms in the church at least on festive and solemn days in the services, and also the mansions of the said church of the mansions of other cathedral churches subject to the penalty contained in this constitution , and you successively inhibited the similar constitution celebrated in another way, and you expressly ordered that no other canon of any other collegiate church in the city, or of the diocese established by the Queen should be able to, or presume to use any, or any alms, or alms similar, dissimilar, or unlike those under the penalty of excommunication and deprivation of benefits, as in the said constitutions which we wish to be regarded as expressed here, it is more broadly contained. Wherefore, on behalf of you and the aforesaid chapter, we were begged, inasmuch as we would design to add the strength of our confirmation to each and every one of the contents of the said constitutions, for a stronger subsistence of the aforesaid constitutions, supplying every deficiency, if anyone might intervene in them. We, therefore, by your and the aforesaid chapter's supplications in this part, as far as we can with God, nodding, the aforementioned constitutions, the tenor of which we wish to be taken as expressed here, and all other and particular things through you, as preferred, having been done, ordered, and approved by that apostolic authority. By our legation and every other authority by which we act, we confirm, approve, and share the present written patronage by supplying all the defects, if any, in the premises, and we resolve that they shall be inviolably observed in perpetual future times, notwithstanding any constitutions, statutes, and customs, and others to the contrary.

Given at Bologna, on the 6th day of December, 1452.

ACT III

The circumspect providence of the apostolic see sometimes tempers the rigor of the law with meekness and indulges, what the sacred canons forbid by the institutions of the grace of kindness, as it knows that, weighing the quality of persons and times, it is healthily expedient in God. Of course, on the part of Bartholomeus deStregonibus and Maria Gasparis deManusiis deRussi, the petition presented to us by the wife of that man, who, not knowing for a long time, that there was some obstacle between them that prevented them from being married to each other. They clandestinely contracted marriage with each other through the words of the present, a carnal union which I have not yet followed; but afterwards it came to their notice that they were united to each other in the fourth degree of consanguinity, for which reason they could not remain in this kind of marriage, not having received the apostolic dispensation over this. And as the same petition subjoined that if a divorce were to take place between the aforesaid Bartholomew and Mary, dissensions, losses, and scandals between them, and their relatives and friends, might very likely arise therefrom.

Wherefore, on behalf of Bartholomew and Mary, we were humbly begged to grant them and any of theirs the benefit of absolution from the general sentence of excommunication, which they had incurred in any way because of a clandestine marriage contract, and that we would agree to provide the grace of a suitable dispensation out of our own kindness. We, therefore, inclined to the supplications of Bartholomew and Mary themselves in this respect, and desiring to provide for the salvation of their souls and to meet such dissensions and scandals as far as we can with God. On this part, we hereby commit and command that the same Bartholomew and Mary and any of their relatives, if they humbly request this, be absolved from this sentence of excommunication, by the aforesaid apostolic authority, in the usual form of the Church, which were to be enjoined by law. Finally, if this is the case, and the said Mary was not abducted for this reason, Bartholomew and Mary, notwithstanding the impediment of the fourth degree of consanguinity of this kind, may remain in the said marriage contracted between them, and proceed to its solemnization in accordance with the institution of the holy mother Church and the custom of the country they may be able freely and lawfully, and be able, by the apostolic authority of the preachers of the dispensation, to decide the legitimacy of such a child to be received out of wedlock. In quorum, et cetera.

> Given at Bologna, May 22, 1453. Bessarion, etc. To the venerable man Sylvester Quirinus of Venice, doctor of decrees, vicar of the most reverend lord archbishop of Ravenna, greetings of sincere charity in the Lord.

ACT IV

Bessarion, by divine mercy, bishop of Tusculan, SRcardinal, popularly called Nicenus, exarchate of Ravenna in the city of Bononia and legate of the apostolic see in the province of Romandiola, to the beloved son of John Anthomus, cleric of Parma, inhabitant of Castri Crepalcori, greetings and sincere charity in the Lord. Honesty of life and manners, and other praiseworthy things. The merits of piety and virtue, on which you are commended to us by a testimony worthy of faith, induce us to render your generous thanks. Since then, just as the series of your petitions offered to us contained, the venerable man Sir John of Siena, doctor of decrees, the reverend father of Sir Guroni Maria Estensis, the trustee of the monastery of Sancti Silvestri of Mantua in the diocese of Mutinensis, the vicar general in the said monastery, a vacant clerical position, or a cleric by beneficence instituted in the Church or plebe of Saints Marie de Brennucio de Crepalcorio, subject to the aforesaid monastery of Sancti Silvestri Cumoleni, has contributed to you the clericate of the aforesaid John, and provided for it. Therefore, on your behalf, it was requested of us that we would like to confer the said clericate to you anew and to provide for it. We, therefore, inclined to your supplications, approving the aforesaid contribution and provision by the authority of our legation, confer upon you the same clergy with all its rights and appurtenances, and we also provide for it, unless at that time given by those present the right, care, government and administration is claimed for another. fully entrusting him to you both in temporal and spiritual matters; commanding each and every farmer, laborer, and others who hold the lands and possessions of the said clergy, that they answer you fully and freely for the fruits, revenues, and proceeds of the same, and that they may be allotted the due effect according to our letter, to whom our present letters have reached, and with the same vigor they have been required singularly or in solid form; in so far as they bring you into the real and corporeal possession of the said clergy and protect and defend the inducted, by removing from thence every unlawful detainer, by controlling any contradictors and rebels by ecclesiastical censure.

  Given at Bologna, on the 18th of April, 1450, in the 13th indictment, in the 4th year of the pontificate of D. Nicholas.

ACTS V

Bessarion, et cetera. Beloved Pasino Melmi of Malchiavel, give us salvation in that way which there is true salvation. The supplication presented to us on your behalf contained: that when in the year 1430 AD you petitioned the cardinal deComite by DL, and other nobles of Malchiavelli were graciously heard, you obtained a decree that the said nobles, who were in number seven heads of families, should in no way be bound to contribute to real personal burdens or together with the men of Roncastal, but they would be understood to be separated from the men of Roncastle, provided that they paid each month to the common chamber of Bononi seventeen pounds, ten solids of Bonon. that is to say, ten pounds and ten solids for each head of the family, as is more seriously stated in the said decree, and asking that when some of the said seven heads, either through impotence or malice, refuse to pay the part touching them, you are disturbed, and you are always compelled to pay the part of such or those who refuse. Wherefore we designed by our special decree to separate the supplicant from the other men of Malchiavel, by touching the loose part to thee. But we who, in the order of our nature, plead with prayers, which we gladly nod, if indeed their intercession seems worthy to you, have committed the aforesaid matter to the examination of our information to the prudent man Paschasius, our hearer, who, having taken careful information, reported to us that what was set forth on your part was true. We, therefore, acting according to your prayers, as far as we can, bearing in mind the aforesaid report, and with the apostolic authority by which we act, confirm the decree that was previously granted to you and others from Malchiavelli, and we grant you anew the Pasino way, and in the future as a payment of fifty solids of Bonon. You must in no way be obliged to pay the tangents for your part, or you can be burdened with the statements of Malchiavelli by some official of the common people of Bologna. Declaring that, having paid the said fifty solids of the Bologna chamber, you, or another in your own name, or your descendants, are in no way worth molesting in any way, or in any order. Commanding the treasurer of the city of Bonn and the defenders of the chamber and others, to whom it pertains, as far as our present decree is concerned, and to cause it to be inviolably observed by others. In whose faith et cetera.

Given etc. on the first day of April, etc.

ACTS VI

Bessarion, et cetera, having chosen for us in Christ, Baltasar the archpriest of Imolens, and Thomas and Christopher, the canons of Imolens, et cetera. We think it worthy and fitting that we should render to them a generous display of grace, to whom the merits of the principal virtues are laudably supported. Since then, as we have received, the archpresbyterate, or the peasants of Saint Mary of Salustria of Imolensis, is vacant with care, and it is known to be vacant at the present time for the fact that Louis Francis [...] ecclesiastical benefice he had obtained peacefully. Desirous of us, dear to us in Christ Emmanuel, once Anthony of Cremon. brother of the Order of Preachers and chaplain to the magnificent lord Thadai Imolæ, et cetera. Even if by free resignation, the scion of the said Louis, or any other person outside the Roman court, made voluntarily in the presence of a reporter and witnesses. And if he has vacated so much time, that his contribution or provision to the apostolic seat of the juxta of the Lateran council, or in any other way legitimately devolved, either specially or generally, exists, and if there is an undecided dispute between some of them, the state of which we wish to be regarded as sufficiently expressed here. Whose fruits, income and proceeds do not exceed forty florins of gold from the Chamber according to the common estimate of the annual value, as the said Emmanuel asserts, with all their rights and appurtenances to the same Emmanuel, with whom, as he asserts, the apostolic authority existed in other ways to accept and receive and that he should be able to retain, until he lives, whatever benefice he has secured, even if it be an archpresbytery, or a priory, or any other dignity, apostolic and our legation, and with every authority by which we act. We have accomplished according to the tenor of the present, and we also provide for him concerning it, deciding from now on to be null and void, if otherwise it happened that an attempt was made on them knowingly or unknowingly. In spite of the fact that the said archpresbyterate, or pleb, through a certain Nicholas Joanni and a canon of Imolens as vicar of the chapter of Imolens, acting in the vacancy of the episcopal see by the episcopal authority of the aforesaid see, may by no means and de facto be said to have been provided by a certain Nicolaus Lippi de Ferris de Faventia and that on the occasion mentioned the same Nicholas presentatively hold and occupy the said archpresbyterate or people: for we want that, notwithstanding the said provision, the same Emmanuel may have the same archpresbytery, or the said people and be able to receive its fruits and revenues with integrity. Wherefore we commit to the discretion of your aforesaid authority, and in the tenor of the present, in so far as by you or another or others the same Emmanuel or his agent in his name receiving into real and corporeal possession the archpresbyterate, or the people of the aforesaid holy Mary of Salustria, and the rights and appurtenances of the same brought in, and by authority defend our inductee, removing from thence any unlawful detainer, making the said Emmanuel, or his agent for him to the same people or archpresbytery, as is the custom, to be admitted to himself or to his agent for the fruits, incomes and proceeds, rights and encumbrances, answerable, any contradictors by checking ecclesiastical censure and other legal remedies. In whose faith, et cetera.

Given at Bologna, June 25, 1450, etc.

ACTS VII

Bessarion, et cetera, to the venerable Father Blasio, abbot SM in Cosmediu, canons of the Holy Spirit of Ravenna. We render ourselves worthy of the duty of legation enjoined upon us, to be anxiously concerned, that in accepting the wishes of those, we may bestow a favorable assent on those who are vacant of the monasteries, churches, and places over which they preside, for the growth and peace of the stables. Of course, on your part, the request offered to us contained that the church of St. Peter in Bresseda was located without care in the territory of Ravenna, which has long been surrounded by marshes and completely fallen into ruins, so that there is no memory to the contrary, that it has ever been of any fruit or value, is vacant to the present. and he was absent for so long, that if his collation looked to any prelate, it was just devolved to the apostolic seat; and that the aforesaid monastery of Saint Mary in Cosmedin has many goods from all sides called the church called Cerium, from which it is easy to see that the said church was subject to your said monastery, although the rights of the monastery itself have for the most part been lost, and you are not able to clearly demonstrate this. Wherefore he subjoined the same request that we should design to unite and incorporate the said church into your monastery. We, therefore, who with unwearied studies favor the righteous, unite the aforesaid church of St. Peter, which is vacant forever, etc. Sending orders to the vicar of the archbishop of Ravenna, and to all the ecclesiastical persons living under our legation, who have been required by their force to bring you in, etc.

Given at Bologna, October 20, 1450.

ACTS VIII

Bessarion, et cetera. Beloved to us in common Christ, the messengers and people of the land of Succidæ and Garnaglon, the Alps of the community of Bononia, greetings and sincere love. Your faith and devotion which you have to the Roman Church and the present state of the city of Bologna; the calamity, moreover, which you endure through various pressures and the barrenness of your own places, induce us to embrace you with gracious favors. For a long time, we have found that the decree of the aforesaid city governor by the reverend Father D. Fantinus Venetus of good memory has been granted to us on behalf of the Holy Roman Church, and the subsequent cancellation of the tenor and continence, that is to say, Fantinus Prothonorarius Venetus on behalf of our most holy lord D. Eugenius Pope IV and the Holy Roman Church Bonon. etc. Governor, beloved to us in Christ common to Massarius and to the people of the land of Succidae and the Alps of Garnaglon, the community of Bologna, salvation in him who is true salvation. Your faith in our calamity was sufficiently diffused by the supplication which you presented to us in the common name; not because all unexpected things are not easily tolerable by a certain nature, but the imminent danger itself brought forth in your piety towards our faith. But when, as you have explained, your houses and common dwellings have all been rooted up and fallen by the flood, and the fall of the mountain where your common residence was situated, and the fertile lands have assumed a barren condition by the said accident, you humbly begged that the people would have no reason to abandon your commons, which we should deign to diminish for one and a half the sum of fifty-two pounds, thirteen solids, four denarii Bonon. which to be paid each year in installments of the salary of the vicars of Capugna, and that at least the necessary salt for you and your commons should be given to you by the bononiese salt farmers for the books of the tribe of Bonon. to the account of the Corbis, as is the case with the other counties of the community of Bonon. because of their poverty. But although we firmly believe your losses and losses, we still want to have all possible information on the matter itself; and we commit the matter to the reverend master treasurer and to the defenders of your common debt Bonon. For they, being sick, confirmed to us that what they had told us in supplication through you was true, and that there were imminent dangers in addition to this, which the mountain itself tends towards the decision: whence they advised us that we should do you a favor: that salt should be given to you in the ratio of baskets for three books A good room, or a cauipa of our salt: and that your common salary, viz., fifty-two pounds, thirteen solids, four denarii, which you are obliged to pay annually for the salary of the Capugnian vicars; which we would remit and reduce to thirty-two pounds and thirteen pounds, four pence Bonon. which are paid annually by you to be held for the salary of the deputies. And the remainder, viz. 20 livres, lest it be prejudiced to the chamber or to other communities, they shall pay in this manner, etc. For a decree was made by the governments of the city of Bologna, and confirmed by a certain most reverend cardinal, otherwise legate of Bologna, that the entrance of the mills of Dacia, which, in proportion to the contingents of the communities of Succidæ, Garnagloni, and Capugnani, should be converted to the account of four solids for the mouth of the said company, for the repair and for the re-appropriation of the baths of Laporetta of the community of Bologna. Now that the constitution itself had already been observed for ten years, and that the repairs were for the most part complete, and that little remained for its completion, they suggested that from the entrance of the aforesaid Dacian mills, for the quota contingent to the said counties, which is collected by the officials deputed for the purpose of the said repair, the said books should be taken for 20 by the full payment of what you were bound to pay for the salary of your vicar, and the remainder of the entrance shall be appropriated for the usual repair of the said baths. For this you advised us, because of your losses, it did not please us in moderation: therefore, desiring to assist you and your calamity in whatever way we can, by the apostolic authority by which we act as a grace to you. We do, we grant, and we grant according to what was meant in the aforesaid report, that the salt should be presented to you for your use by the Bonon salt cane. for the three books of Bonon. inasmuch as you are obliged to pay only for the salary of the Vicar of Capugnan, the aforesaid thirty-two pounds, thirteen solidi, and four denarii of Bologna, but the other 20 pounds are only paid for the entrance appointed for the repair of the baths by him, or by those who are appointed for a similar exaction, as more fully expressed above it is; commanding the treasurer of Bonon's chamber. which will be for the time being, to the defenders, the contractors, and the surviving salt, the deputy drivers of Capugna, the officials assigned to the enforcement of the said entrance for the repair of the baths and to each and every one of our other officials and the common people of Bologna whom he looks or may look to in the future, as long as they keep this our grace , and let them be observed from time to time by others. In whose faith the present grant of ours is decreed, and sealed with our round seal:

> Given at Bologna in the palace of our residence, on the fifteenth day of February 1452, in the first year of the pontificate of our most holy lord Eugenius Pope, et cetera.

Acts IX

After the granting of the decree and annulment, the venerable soldier D. Nicolaus de Sanatis of the city of Bologna was taken by apostolic authority as count Palatine, and in the title of his county the place called Laporetta, with all its appurtenances and jurisdictions, and also with the vicarage of the said lands, and by the payment of four solidi for every mouth of men and persons existing in the lands themselves, as they had formerly been wont to pay for the mill of the chamber of Bologna, he obtained the provision by the same authority, as is clearly established in the apostolic letters drawn up therefrom and exhibited before us. And since there has often been a dispute between the aforesaid noble count and respectable soldier on the one side, and the deputies appointed for the time being to the government of the world on the other, and also the communities and people of the same on the other side, and there is also a controversy about the present occasion of the payment of the salary of the said vicarage, and also of the payment twenty pounds, which the aforesaid communities, and the men for their mouths, have been wont to pay in certain past years for the repair of the baths of Laporetta, for the payment of which the aforesaid universities and men assert that they are not bound by the pre-inserted decree by the authority of the said lands: therefore we, desiring to cut off the materials of the jurgis, and most affecting to provide for the peace, rest and tranquility of our subjects, we confirm by our present decree, that the aforesaid universities and their men are bound to pay for all that and all that on the occasion of the aforesaid slaughtered for their mouths the chamber of Bonn, of all the rest, each of eleven pounds of Bonon. and not further to the aforesaid Nicholas, the aforesaid count and soldier from the time of the grant of the apostolic authority made to him on this side, from calculating the whole of the said sum which the said universities and men were found to have been paid to the aforesaid Nicholas, they shall effectively pay without any diminution; that eleven pounds should be given up from the profit of the said county for the repair of the baths of Laporetta, as it appears from the apostolic letters that the same was granted, and also that the said universities and men should pay for the salary of the said university every year, according to the usual order to the vicars appointed for the time, and to the deputation of impostors by having the means for this purpose, fifty-two pounds, thirteen solids, and four pence plenary from the remainder thereof, which for all the time past and up to the time of the apostolic provision, as is aforesaid, the said universities and men were bound to pay on the said occasion the remission, deliverance, and by granting the exemption. And moreover, we confirm and approve the aforesaid decree, inserted by us, duly inspected in all its parts, beyond the aforesaid authority of our legation, and we also approve of the new writings in it, commanding the lord treasurer, the defenders of the city of Bonon. and to others to whom he looks, both present and future, to observe all the aforesaid things, and to cause them to be observed inviolably by others.

> Given at Bologna, et cetera. on November 20, 1450, indictment 3, the pontificate of Nicolai, Pope Vanno IV.

The Scriptorium Project is the work of a small group of lay people of various apostolic churches who are interested in the preservation, transmission, and translation of the works of the early and medieval church. Our efforts are to make the works of the church fathers accessible to anyone who might have an interest in Christian antiquities and the theological, philosophical, and moral writings that have become the bedrock of Western Civilization.

To-date, our releases have pulled from the Greek, Syriac, Georgian, Latin, Celtic, Ethiopian, and Coptic traditions of Christianity, and have been pulled from sundry local traditions and languages.

Other Selections from the Byzantine Church Series:

Treatise on Sobriety by Nicephorus the Solitary (Apr. 2007)
Select Acts by John Bessarion (Oct. 2008)
Sermons by Nestorius of Constantinople (May 2009)
Theophrastus by Aeneas of Gaza (Apr. 2011)
Treatise on Prayer by St. Evargius of Ponticus (May 2011)
The Lausiac History by St. Palladius of Galatia (Mar. 2013)
Letter on the Fall of Constantinople by Isidore of Kiev (Oct. 2013)
The Hesychast by Gregory of Sinai (June 2015)
Selected Laws by Justinian I, Emperor of Rome (July 2018)
Exhortation to Monks Ordained in India by St. John of Karpathos (March 2021)
Fragments of 'Chronicle' by Hippolytus of Thebes (May 2023)
The Life of the Blessed Theotokos by Epiphanius Monachus (July 2023)
Letters of Nestorius by Nestorius of Constantinople (Sept. 2023)

SELECT ACTS